PIANO
VOCAL
GUITAR

MELISSA
ETHERIDGE
FEARLESS LOVE

ISBN 978-1-4234-7608-5

HAL•LEONARD®
CORPORATION
7777 W. BLUEMOUND RD. P.O. BOX 13819 MILWAUKEE, WI 53213

In Australia Contact:
Hal Leonard Australia Pty. Ltd
4 Lentara Court
Cheltenham, Victoria, 3192 Australia
Email: ausadmin@halleonard.com.au

Visit Hal Leonard Online at
www.halleonard.com

FEARLESS LOVE

Words and Music by
MELISSA ETHERIDGE

THE WANTING OF YOU

Words and Music by
MELISSA ETHERIDGE

COMPANY

Words and Music by
MELISSA ETHERIDGE

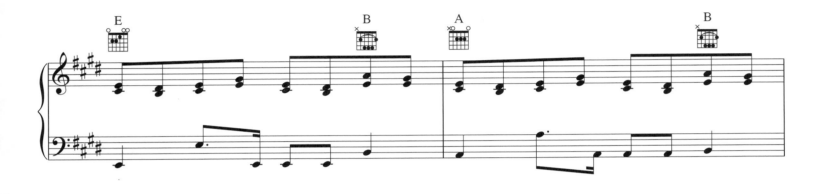

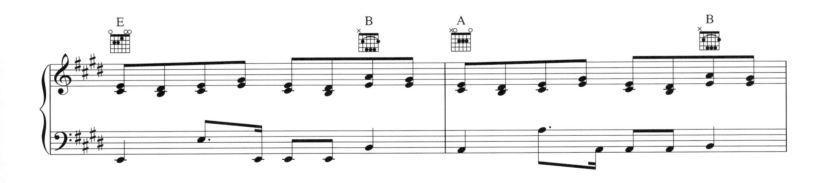

If you ask ___ me, I will

MISS CALIFORNIA

Words and Music by
MELISSA ETHERIDGE

DRAG ME AWAY

Words and Music by
MELISSA ETHERIDGE

39

There's no dark that can o-ver-come a flame, __ there's no

force that can drag __ me __ a - way. __

INDIANA

Words and Music by
MELISSA ETHERIDGE

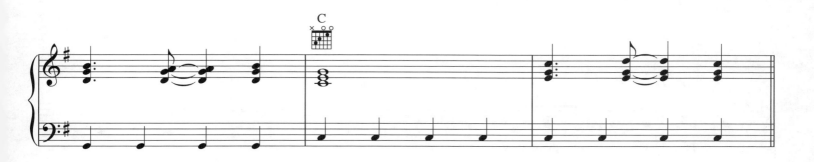

She tend-ed bar ____ in ____ New ____ York Ci - ty.

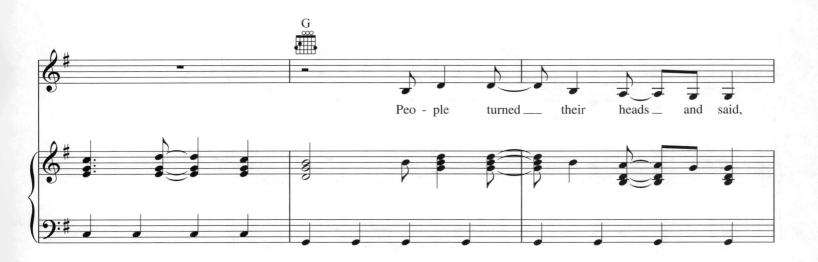

Peo - ple turned ____ their heads ____ and said,

NERVOUS

Words and Music by
MELISSA ETHERIDGE